INVISIBLE
Walls

How to create deeper connections through
the purity of experiences

INVISIBLE
Walls

How to create deeper connections through
the purity of experiences

Stephanie Zorn Kasprzak

Printed in the United States of America

Are you looking for deeper connections and a more meaningful life?

This book is written for
my 20-year-old self who
always wanted to be a writer...

Never give up

Picks & Shovels

By Stephanie Zorn

They are companions who navigate my soul and tickle the
sanity which crawls in my mind of winding rivers.

They are my architects who square-dance through evergreen
solitude where silence is my majesty.

They hollow the dungeons and free the soldiers.

They are divine subconscious.

Creating an awakening so brightly congruent that
they leave my navigated barracks healed.

Cover: Tucker Publishing House team

Editing: Wynn Editing and Tara Tucker

Paperback ISBN: 979-8-9859565-6-6

Hardcover ISBN 979-8-9859565-7-3

Library of Congress Control Number: 2022911614

Contents

Foreword

For my mom...

Okay, fine, I'll start.

I was born on Mother's Day in 2003. If you ask my mom, she'll tell you I was named after Maya Angelou. Courtesy of my mom - I was raised on the Indigo Girls, The Beatles, and Bob Dylan. I was raised on traveling, loving my life, and doing the right thing. My mom and I share the same love for that first cup of coffee in the morning right after yoga. She took me to my first protest when I was 12 or 13, and she's taken me to countless concerts, even though I know she didn't always want to. I get my spunk, my ambition, my desire to help people and my toughness from my mom. She's the funniest when she's had a glass or two of wine or some Bailey's. She always brightens up the room and sees the best in everything. She's always been supportive of my dreams to leave this town, but I know deep down that she's dreading my "move out" day. She's wondering who she'll rant to after a long day? Who she'll share her accomplishments with? Who she'll have constant support from? Who will always be there? But I also know that she knows deep down, I'm wondering *who I'll rant to after a long day, who I'll share my accomplishments with, who I'll have constant support from, and who will always be there*. Where would I be without my mom?

Maya ♡

Introduction

During this time of COVID-19 and all of our emphasis on social media, zoom calls, and distance from one another, the world has become lonelier. In early 2020, so much of the world, along with the United States, went home to quarantine, facing a global pandemic. At the time, it seemed that this might linger for a few weeks, perhaps a month, then life would resume. People went out very little, limited their connections with others and spent time only with the loved ones who filled their household. People went inward, and for many, that meant being alone. Alone with our screens – binge-watching shows on television, following and posting on social media, participating in endless zoom calls – all in an effort to try and remain connected with others in the unprecedented and completely unknown time. This invisible wall is what we've adjusted to after such a lengthy time and with no end in sight. When people retreated home, there was no knowledge of how long that might linger. As of this writing, there are still so many who continue their lives in this way with COVID-19 still alive and moving its way across the United States.

This invisible wall has left a void with people feeling lonely and disconnected from one another. It shows in the level of discourse between people these days; the protests revolving around social justice, the political divides about election fraud, vaccines, and mask mandates. The truth has become what is read on social media and not what is the reality around us based on research, data, and science.

This is not a book about all that. It is a book about our ability to rebound, reconnect, and have deep connections with others despite difficult circumstances that we face in life. Exploring these deeper connections is a way to pay homage to the simple and often overlooked relationships we have that are so critically important. It is not only connections with people that bring fulfillment to our lives but also experiences and exposure to the world around us that can give a broader perspective.

It is important to begin to document the many aspects of COVID-19 and how it has changed our lives. In reflecting on how it has changed my life, this book explores the many relationships and experiences I've had that allowed me to have deep connections and realize the love and peace that life has to offer. This love has taken many forms and has shaped the person I am today. The purity of love is important to recognize and helps us to feel less lonely and insecure. It brings us to deeper connections.

My hope is that from this book, you will gather from these collective experiences new ways to look at connecting on a deeper level, bringing you peace and a more meaningful life.

Moments

By Stephanie Zom-Kasprzak

One day we will look back on all these little moments and
smile at the lifetime in between.

Because these are the moments that have
become the "us" that I adore.

The "us" I don't want to give up.

The "us" that is gentle and kind — inspiring and equal —
balanced and complementary.

It is nothing (no expectations, no pressure) and yet

everything (all that I want).

Some days you leave me alone to ponder these moments.

To make sure they are real and not just dandelion
wishes floating in the breeze.

And as sure as the sun is shining on my face,
I am smiling, thinking of them.

Sometimes forgotten but near to my heart.

I write them for you, so you know my handwriting.

The intimacy of penmanship has been lost on some.

But one day, we may not remember, so I must share,
so you know of their grand impression.

Chapter 1

For Tim

"Life waits for no one."

Our family grew up in Michigan. In November, sometimes you get those miraculous days that give you one last taste of summer before the winter sets in. Today was a day like this. It was a Monday, but one of those days when you just felt the need to call in sick to work and be outdoors. The leaves were yellow, and with the harvest fields of fall all around, our part of the world had a golden tint. When a sudden wind came through, the leaves fell like snow. The ladybugs were fluttering about one last day before they disappeared again, to wherever it is they go in winter. It was perfect.

The day took a turn from the very start. My husband and I were on the tail end of our marriage by then, and the silence was only broken by a fight. I don't even know what we argued about that morning, but the last words out of my mouth expressed a serious dislike for talking to him at all. I got in the car and drove off to work.

I was about a mile down the road, and my cell phone rang – it was my mom. I don't remember her exact words, but they went something like this...

Come back home. Your dad needs help. They found your brother on the floor.

I have two brothers. Then there's me. We are all five years apart – good planning on my parents' part to separate the cost of college. This also meant that we weren't terribly close growing up. My older brother, Tim, and I became closer as we aged.

FOR TIM

Tim was the type of guy who was always there. The rock of his family and my enduring and goofy older brother. He wasn't a man rich with money, but he would share all he had. He was a hard worker, carried two jobs, and gave his kids all he had. That's how our parents raised us. To be solid and dependable, work hard for everything, and always provide for your kids and family. All of my siblings aimed to raise our families like we had been brought up.

He loved to tend his garden and spent possibly too much time outside. There was always extras grown in Tim's garden to donate to the food pantry, which I ran as a non-profit executive. He loved being outside in the garden, and the process of planting, weeding, harvesting, and sharing his yield fed his spirit and many others as well. We shared a love for getting our hands in the soil and also for the fall season – especially on days like today.

After my mom's call, I immediately turned the car around, drove back home, and pulled into my brother's house. Our family lived on a dead-end country road with a creek right across from our houses. I walked into the house my dad pumping my brother's chest with a look I'd never seen before. My dad is the pillar of our family. He never waivers. We always thought he could fix anything, knew everything, and was trusted. I saw his face filled with fear and desperation for his firstborn son. I leaned down next to him and touched my brother's arm. I said, "Dad. He's cold."

He said, "I don't really know how to do this..." and I started to help. In all honesty, I didn't know either. My mom came in the front door, phone in hand. They had called 9-1-1, and she was trying to reach Tim's wife, who left for work earlier that morning.

We lived in a small, rural township, so when the sirens blew, people paid attention to where it was going. A little bit nosey and out of care and caution, people watched the direction of the firetrucks. Our little one-lane dead-end road quickly became filled with noise and movement of people we grew up with and knew. My dad was well-known as a township elected official, and the volunteer firefighters were all familiar in one way or another – friends, neighbors, they all knew the address. They knew where they were going. They quickly ushered my dad and I out of the way, replaced by machines and fresh arms to continue pumping.

He was young and healthy, they said. I held his arm and sometimes touched his face as they worked. He was still cold. During that situation, it seemed like time moved in slow motion. The people came in and out. They pumped. They whispered. They worked in a very focused and determined manner. Like nothing else matters. He's so young; we must get him back.

My brother's wife arrived home. She started talking to him. She asked the firefighters how long they had been working on him. 45 minutes. She asked them not to stop yet.

Many of my uncles farm the land that surrounds our homes. Taking advantage of the day, they were out harvesting in nearby fields. But this day, the scenery was different. Now they are all congregated in the front yard. The local sheriff had since arrived. Our neighbors began to walk down the road to inquire about the situation. My brother's wife had her parents come quickly. I called my husband, who would not answer. As we congregated in the front yard while the firefighters worked, I could faintly hear my brother's wife talking to Tim, pleading for him to come back. My mom looks at me and says, "what about the kids?"

At some point through this process, a feeling settles in. The feeling that it's just been too long. Your world shifts from it'll be okay, to what do we do now? ....Like the rug is being pulled out from under you. like this beautiful day was just too good to be true.

Finally, the firefighters called the doctor. Then they called the time of death. I don't know what time it was exactly. I just remember a gust of wind that came through at that moment, as I was standing in the front yard while the leaves fell like snow.

There are feelings that you get and a level of sadness that sets in when you see people you've never seen cry before or when your parent's hearts get broken. There's a cry that lets out sometimes that comes from a place deep in your soul. I remember these feelings vividly and write them so as to never forget.

I remember the mortuary van pulling up. We all went inside for one final look. Perhaps for closure or validation that soon this sweet face would be gone forever. You never forget the black body bag coming out the door on a stretcher and into the van.

Then we talked about the best way to tell the kids. We orchestrated who would get them and what they would say on the ride home. Their best friends arrived and their boyfriends came to give comfort. We all rolled back on our heels for a collective sigh.

I needed a break, so I walked the long way home through the woods, then sat on my back steps and sobbed until there was no moisture left in my face. The next few days were quiet. I left the front porch light on every night just in case he could still find his way home somehow.

The food and condolences from many people poured in. Each night, our entire family ate together and looked through old photographs that best captured my brother's spirit. We planned a funeral, created a video of his life, and picked his favorite songs. The video resurfaces from time to time, and we watch and laugh at my lack of technical savvy, his weird haircuts and vintage clothes, and the moments that made his life. So many people came out to celebrate his life, and that taught me a great lesson.

Do you ever wonder if you died tomorrow, who would come and pay their respects at your funeral? Well, Tim would have been overwhelmed by the attention. You see, he was a humble and loyal man. He kept good friends for many years, worked hard to earn respect and provided stability for his family. That week was brutal. After the funeral, we gathered once again around the table with Tim's ashes in the middle. We drank, laughed and listened to our parents' stories of when they were young because you're never promised tomorrow.

We never really drank much, but on that day, it was a release. My mom told me of dates with my dad at the Peppermint Club and how she accidentally shot my Aunt Rita in the ass one time. We talked about my brother's love for a good bonfire by the creek blaring Bob Seger. We spoke of his heartaches, his successes, and his dreams.

You see, my brother was 49 when he died. He worked hard all of his life and was nearing retirement at an early age. He loved hiking, camping and being outdoors. He had traveled many places across the United States, seeing gorgeous sceneries and picturesque state and national parks. He and I shared a great passion for seeing beautiful places in all their glory. While remembering the simple moments; like a random warm November day when the yellow leaves fell like snow. There is a perspective that nature gives you that can make the biggest problems seem small. The largest projects seem manageable. Although my brother had his struggles, nature always provided solace and peace to navigate his way through it and come out the other side a better person.

Find your solace and what gives you peace.

Sometimes we take for granted and overlook the deep connection we can have with our siblings. These are people who literally have known us for as long as we've existed and yet don't see the imprint they make based on this longevity in our lives. Personalities don't mesh well, resentments happen over time, and lives just go in different directions. I get that. But no matter the invisible wall, try to keep connections with those who know us deeply. Like our siblings, because one day they might not be there to sit on the back porch and lament about our teenagers. That was the last interaction I had with my brother.

FOR TIM

On my brother's bucket list was to hike the Appalachian Trail at the age of 50. Yes, 50. He was almost there and had started making plans. One day we'll take him there and spread some ashes along the way.

Take a moment now and reflect on your life. Do you have regret? Are there things you want to do? Many people have a bucket list but never make it out the door. Take this story as a reminder not to wait. Don't spend time planning for tomorrow what you should be doing today. Now is the time.

Write a list of personal goals for your life. The legacy you'd like to leave, your proverbial footprint on the world. Once you have your goals in place, make it your life's purpose to keep making your mark, one day at a time. You never know when it might be your last.

Chapter 2

The Ground on Which You Stand

"Stay true to yourself."

Our family never really traveled much when I was young. That is by no means a slight on my family or childhood; it just wasn't something that people did as much as they do now. My dad was an accountant, and my mom stayed at home to raise our family until we were old enough, and then she went to work in the elementary school we attended. We just always stayed close to home and had just as much fun playing outside with our cousins in the fields, woods and by the creek.

I remember there was a time or two when we went to Lancaster, Pennsylvania. My dad had a business trip and the family tagged along in our station wagon with wood paneling on the side and no seat belts. The kids loaded up in the back and sat cross-legged the entire way. As we drove to Lancaster, we saw the horse and buggies of the Amish traveling on the road. Cool. The hotel had a pool. That is the extent of my childhood memories regarding travel.

That is until I was 17. In high school, we were required to take language credits for graduation. I took German because our family ancestry traced back to Germany. I joined the German Club at some point during my high school career and in my senior year they organized a trip to Germany. In our post 9/11 world, it seems hard to imagine a high school field trip to another country. Moreover, what teacher in their right mind would take a large group of teenagers overseas to a country famous for Oktoberfest? But our fearless German teacher, Herr Ott, did it – called the trip – organized the visits – and I was going.

I had never been away from my parents, never been on a plane, and certainly didn't have a passport. Over spring break of 1988, I was headed to Germany. I had taken four years of German language in school, so I felt somewhat prepared. What I didn't realize then is that it would instill in me a love of travel and begin to formulate the ideals in life on which I stand today.

Let me tell you...being a teenager going overseas without your parents was a TRIP! After the plane ride and bus route that seemed to last a lifetime, we arrived at our hotel, checked in and got situated. It felt like we had been sitting for days, so we ventured out of the hotel to stretch our legs and see what was around us. Just think a minute about being a teenager in a country with no drinking age – so our first stop was to McDonald's across the street, where we became ecstatic to order a beer off the menu.

The trip included a boat ride down the Rhine River. Visits to many extravagant German castles, the mountains and many beloved historic sites. One of my favorites was going to Austria and being on the site where they filmed "The Sound of Music," where we enjoyed a gazebo stroll and photo shoot. There were three main stops that stood out in my mind and reshaped my life as I knew it. These included Dachau, visiting the Berlin Wall, and going through Checkpoint Charlie to enter East Berlin. Yes, our group traveled to the communist-occupied city of East Berlin. Who approved THIS?! But we were young, free, and in another country, so we took in every moment.

Dachau was one of the concentration camps that killed more than 40,000 people during the Holocaust. The day was dreary – it was rainy and cool since it was April. We walked through the empty barracks with line after line of wooden bunk beds where people slept. We walked along the barbed wire that lined the perimeter. We walked through large, open cement rooms that we understood to be former gas chambers. We saw the steel furnaces. It was silent and shocking as we listened to the tour guide tell of the unimaginable environment that people experienced. At the gates, it read: "Arbeit Macht Frei" – work sets you free. But for many, it simply didn't. Dachau was liberated by United States forces in April 1945. At the age of 17, I really had a difficult time understanding the holocaust, but the visit to Dachau opened my eyes to brutality and discrimination against the human spirit. The part of my soul that protests against oppression and defies hatred was born on that day visiting Dachau.

The Berlin Wall is likely something that people who are younger than the Generation-X era have literally never heard of. That there was a wall erected to separate a city into two opposing political ideals may sound strange. However, today we do the same thing, sometimes with walls and often times without. The Berlin Wall was not an invisible one; it was a literal one that separated the City of Berlin from 1961 to 1989 during the Cold War.

Like border crossings can be now, in the post-9/11 era where patrols with guns blocked the passage from West to East Berlin, the Wall acted as the divider. The tour group went to the Branden-burg Gate and was able to see and touch the Berlin Wall. It was 1988, only one brief year before the Wall would fall, and the western side of the wall was littered with graffiti. A type of vandalism mixed with art that might seem to have some poetic justice to those on the right side of it. I picked up a piece of the Wall and put it in my pocket, paying no mind that our next trip was to East Berlin.

As we entered the checkpoint, there continued a feeling of divisiveness. A sharp contrast and intentional effort to separate people, worlds and cultures. My 17-year-old brain thought it interesting that a city could work so hard to be in two pieces. It really didn't make sense to me at the time, but as history often repeats itself, there can be parallels made with our country today. Because not all history is a good history, and at times not all places are beautiful.

The Brandenburg Gate marked the crossing from West to East Berlin. It is a marvelous structure and very stately to see. The infamous Checkpoint Charlie is where we would cross the border into the east. We rode on a large tour bus full of students and chaperones, with all of our souvenirs and belongings from a full day of site-seeing. We stopped at the checkpoint and watched armed guards everywhere. In short, they check the cars, buses, bikes and all vehicles for items not appropriate for crossing.

"I'm certain a tour bus of teenagers from America was not a red flag at all," thought my 17-year-old self. Writing this now just gives me pause. Hindsight is best right? The guards entered the bus; there were two or three, if my mind serves me correctly. They went by each person, checking bags as they went. We all watched with a small dose of fear. At some point, as they drew near to my row, I wondered if it was a bad idea to pick up that piece of the Berlin Wall that now rests in my pocket. My palms started to sweat. The guards passed my space in an uneventful fashion. I was relieved. Row by row, they proceeded; I thought we were in the clear, that they would move along with no issue. A gentle reminder, this was a time before cell phones, earbuds, or technology devices of most kinds. So, we watched and listened as the process unfolded.

When the guards went to the back of the bus, they got stuck with two kids in our group. They went through their bags. They took their bags and left the bus with them. Then they came back to take the students with them. We started to chatter – WHAT was going on?! Herr Ott escorted the students and the guards with their guns off the bus. An unsettling feeling spread throughout the bus. Herr Ott was our RIDE! The one who really knows German. The guy in charge. What if he doesn't come back?

It felt like an eternity. In reality, it was probably 30 minutes; I don't really know. In the end, the students bought Playboy Magazines in the west and took them through in their bags. Unknown to them that was a bad idea. I hope one of them one day writes a story of what happened to them for real. But to us, it became an urban legend at the school for the rest of the year, and these two kids had some serious street credibility in German Club. I don't think the high school ever went back again. A year later, the Berlin Wall came down. I keep my piece of the Wall, along with the empty McDonald's beer can, in my memory box, as well as a lifetime of impressions.

One of the biggest impressions left from this trip was rebellion. Rebellion against oppression and hate. Seeing Dachau and a Wall that divides people changed my worldview and the ground on which I stand forever. Hate and discrimination became ideals to fight against in daily life and in the bigger picture. This lasting impression set the tone for my life to come, even though I didn't know it then. Beliefs rooted deeply in experience and feeling change us forever.

THE GROUND ON WHICH YOU STAND

This has taken shape throughout my life in many ways. As I went through college, we attended a protest against war, supported gay rights, and became vehement feminists. The environment and social justice issues became platforms for our lives. Seeing those walls in Germany provided me with purpose...to realize their place and work like hell to break them down. It has been my life's work. Find your ground and stand firmly upon it.

Chapter 3

Strangers

"Everyone Matters"

When I went to college, I decided at one point that I wanted to be a poet. Then I visited my advisor, who said, "Well, that's great, but how are you going to LIVE?" So, I changed direction, moving into a journalism major. It was still writing, but a way to use it to make a living, the best of both worlds, I thought. In my last year of college, I took a class that required me to do volunteer work at a local non-profit organization. So, I engaged with an agency that provided a 24/7 crisis hotline to help people with a variety of issues, food, housing, or just a friendly ear to talk to. I went through volunteer training and then signed up to work the midnight shift once a week on the crisis hotline. I remember taking calls to set up appointments for the food bank and giving people resources for the local homeless shelters, but there was one night that changed my life.

There was a small office space where the crisis line was. A telephone with the walls all around littered with phone numbers, event flyers, and inspirational sayings to keep volunteers engaged and coming back. On that night, I arrived, taking a look to see what was new. The volunteer coordinator called to see how it was going for me, "So far, all is well." I took a few phone calls and handled them with what I thought was ease. Then a call came in. Truthfully, I cannot remember if it was a man or woman's voice, but that matters little. They expressed feeling helpless like there was nothing left for them in this world.

Quickly I realized the depth of the voice and their struggle to want to live. It was a suicide call. I felt totally inadequate. I wasn't sure how to be prepared for this — I thought back to our training — "make a contract" is what I remember. We talked for a bit about the circumstances of their life that got them to this point. The challenges of school, the loneliness of being away from home, and the feeling of being different from their peers. Sometimes they didn't eat for days, and sleep was precarious. It all seemed unmanageable and hopeless; would it ever turn around?

They had a plan. When you hear someone describe how they plan to take their life, it stops you in your tracks. I felt inadequate, so I made a contract. Although my shift was only four hours long, we talked for many hours. And if I'm being honest, I did little talking and more listening. Listening to people holds tremendous value, more than we can ever know. I can never know what happened to that person after we hung up the phone that night. We made a contract, a pact between us two, that there would be the next day. And then my shift was over.

That was the call that changed my path forever. This call was from a stranger who only needed me to listen and hear them. I decided to begin my career working in the non-profit sector. This passion has led to a beautifully meaningful career and life of helping people. Being there for strangers in their time of need, being kind and sometimes just listening. I have a career full of stories that give credence to this ideal. It truly makes a difference in our world, however little or big it seems.

That brings me to the story of a perfect stranger. A lovely and sweet senior citizen who was on a list to receive a Christmas basket for the homebound. This was her lone visit during the holiday. You see, she was recently discharged from the hospital after an illness and lived alone in her home. She was on her own with no family members in close proximity and it was becoming more of a challenge for her to live alone. So, when some-one called to send her a Christmas basket, she wel-comed the help.

I knocked on the door and waited. It took her some time to get there. I could hear her foot-steps, so I waited patiently. She opened the door and had a big smile on her face; she was happy for the visit. She invited me to sit and I listened to her talk about the health issues and hospitalization. She asked, "What is in the basket?" so I opened it; I showed her the meal, the toiletry items and gave her a present.

She opened the present with pride. It was a beautiful blanket. She said how kind it was to visit and bring her the basket because she wasn't antic-ipating any company over Christmas. She loved the blanket. I told her how a local company did a blanket drive to make sure all of our seniors had a present of warmth during the cold winter months. She began to cry.

She explained to me how she worked for that very company for decades. She explained her job and how much it supported her life and family over the years. She cried tears of joy because she felt less alone. Knowing that those co-workers she had spent so much time with throughout her career still made the time to be there for her, even though she was not working there. It was a connection that brought her a smile on Christmas Eve and I was the vessel sent to connect the dots to her past life.

It is important to gently remind ourselves to reach out to complete strangers sometimes – in the line at the store, volunteering at a nonprofit agency, or just making small talk with someone whom we've lost touch with. Random kindness makes deep connections whether we know it or not. In the end, it doesn't matter if we know it or not; it is only critical that we do it to keep our connection with the human spirit.

Chapter 4

The Parenting Journey

"We do it all to give them everything."

I believe that everyone has walls they have built around them. For one reason or many, there are events that happen in our lives that lead us to close off a part of ourselves to the rest of the world. However, we know they exist. I think of it as self-preservation; walls that have been built to protect ourselves from vulnerability. From people really seeing us. Good or bad, I don't really know, I guess you can look at it both ways.

I also believe that there are pieces of our experiences that we get to keep all to ourselves. These are true gifts of memory, only held as long as we can remember them. I call them "Walter Mitty moments." In the Secret Life of Walter Mitty (spoiler alert), there is a photographer who takes pictures of spectacular moments, ones that others may never experience, and publishes them for all to see and experience. Near the end, there is a moment when the photographer, who has been sitting for a long time, is waiting for a snow leopard to come so he can capture the moment. When the snow leopard emerges, he watches in silence and never takes a photograph because some moments he chooses to keep for himself. So, for all of the photographs we take that sit in albums or in the phone gallery, it's the ones that stick in our minds that really matter. At least for as long as we can remember them.

All of that being equal, it does seem important to be as authentic with people who are close in our lives and experience that vulnerability. That is, after all, how we achieve closeness. I have this recurring dream when I have very anxious moments in my life. I'm not talking about general nervousness but super anxious moments when I feel there is no way out. I recall having this recurring dream most when I was pregnant with my children. To me, the act of being pregnant and giving birth to human beings who would need you forever to nurture them was a heavy burden for me to internalize. The by-product of this anxiety was this dream.

The dream is simple and goes something like this. I am in the middle of an ocean, treading water. It is blue everywhere. The water is blue, the sky is blue, and nothing else is around. Although I can swim, I'm not a huge fan of water, so I belabor as I tread, thinking, "How am I going to get out of this?" There is nothing in this vast ocean with me to grab onto, so all I can do is tread and fret over my next steps. Then suddenly, a massive brick wall comes right out of the ocean and rises up high into the air. Because it's a brick wall, it gives me nothing to hold onto. I try to work my fingers into the crevasses to no avail. It was of no use; the wall didn't matter.

That's the dream. Perhaps that's the whole point. Walls don't help. The fact of the matter is that I was having those babies, and there was no turning back. I put my mind towards being the very best mom ever. No questions asked.

My children are the absolute greatest gifts of my life and my deepest connections. Anything that important, I don't do half-assed. So, if I put my whole heart into it, I know it is a great passion that will span my entire life. Period. In this type of situation, it is easier for me to let my walls down because vulnerability allows you to unlock your true self and I wanted that as a parent.

Are there people in your life or activities that you pursue that always remain on the surface? Of course, there are; it is unrealistic to find deep connections all the time. There are, however, deep connections in simple moments. But do they matter? Sure, in some way, they do. However, they aren't the deep connections that help us break down those walls. Those are the meaningful ones. If you are striving for a true and authentic life, look no further than those deep connections. The ones that allow you to let it all down and be true to yourself. Keep those close and work to nurture them.

It is not only people with whom we can have these deep connections. It can be a career. Finding passion in your career is, to me, considered a calling. It is a path you were meant to find, foster, and put your whole heart into. I knew that helping people was my calling, but it didn't come like a light bulb and just turn on. I volunteered and found an interest, turned it into a job, liked said job, and put my whole heart into it. This journey has led to many deep connections. I spent time growing and evolving into the work, making it eventually my career. I became good at it because it fueled my passion. I knew at some point I would stay in the field because I loved it, and every day was like a gift. Over the years, I became increasingly adaptable to it because when you love something, you are flexible to the ever-changing moments that can happen. You adjust and keep going. You never give up. This mindset can ring true to all aspects of life.

I approached parenting the same way. You have to be adaptable to allow people to become their true, authentic selves. In raising kids, yes, they take on some of the parental characteristics, but you are not raising children to be YOU. You are raising children to be themselves. Not everyone agrees with my style of parenting, and it definitely puts a wedge between myself and the father of my children.

But I believe in it with all my heart, and that's how it has worked out. I consider myself an organic parent. I let my kids find out who they were by following their own paths. I realize that this probably sounds dangerous for young children, so let me elaborate.

When our children were babies and toddlers, I emphasized to them the acts of kindness and positivity. I did this through action, both with them and with others. I took great care to provide structure for them when they were little. I also made certain that I showed kindness and positivity in my everyday living. After all, kids will mirror their environment. This played out in random acts of kindness to the babysitter, bank teller, our family members, and all around. This is not to say that I didn't have rotten days, I did, but even on those, I tried to see the bright side. Not only did that instill in my children a defense mechanism to get through the tough times, but it also helped my own mindset to be resilient. After all, parenting is hard.

As they grew and entered school on their own journey, I let the reins go a bit. This is not to say that there wasn't structure or discipline in their lives; they had both. When I grew up, my father used some alternate methods in parenting that I thought were important and memorable, and they also WORKED. The best example I remember is when I was in elementary school. I stole a little girl's ring on the bus and got caught. My dad was so disappointed in me for stealing, and I can still feel that moment to this day. He did not yell, scold me, put me on time out, or ground me. He simply was disappointed. From that day on, I did not lie or steal. I learned the power of disappointment from someone I loved. It changed me. In fact, I never remember my dad as a strict disciplinarian. He let us make our mistakes, and he aimed to better align us with Catholic values as we had those issues. I was never grounded or scolded, or paddled (except by my 5th-grade teacher) my parents showed us the way through action because most times, actions speak louder than words.

I also worked to teach my children how to be resourceful. We live in such a throw-away society that I felt it was important to provide ways to counter that mindset. We need to be creative and use what we have at our disposal to access what we need instead of just simply going out and buying it. So, when the children were young, we learned some ways to recycle, reuse, and create based on the things we have around us. My youngest was in 4-H, a national youth development program that teaches kids life skills, and she learned how to sew, create Christmas ornaments, and make a compelling public speech. She reused material to sew clothing, curtains, and pillows. She picked pine-cones, leaves, and flowers to assemble oneof-a-kind ornaments and keep-sakes. These are the pieces with the best memories that we still show-case today.

The children learned how to make decisions on their own. Through simple random acts like picking out their own clothes to match their identity and style all the way to getting tattoos as a statement of purpose. Children learn how to think through daily tasks and learn their process for decision making. They learn to look at the impact their decisions will have on their lives and the lives of others around them, continually building on the foundation of kindness and positivity. Learning lessons the hard way is another by product of organic parenting. As children grow into teens, they begin to have more adult problems, so teaching along the way the consequences of your actions can sometimes be a hard lesson.

Throughout their childhood, I fostered a love to travel and see beautiful places to foster freedom and independence. It is a wide-open feeling to jump in the car or hop on a plane with some clothes and cash to explore places you've never seen before. We traveled to museums, state and national parks, lakes, and oceans, along with big cities. As I loved nature for the peace and serenity it provides to me; I wanted to instill that love in my children. Not to force it, but for them to take it and use it however they feel is right for them, up to and including never. Since they were young, I've exposed them to state and national parks across the United States. In 2016, it was the 100-year anniversary of the National Park System. We made five trips to parks and these were some of the most memorable times.

At Mammoth Caves in Kentucky, we experienced the darkness of the underground tunnels with the bats and translucent spiders included. We hiked the three-dune challenge at Indiana State

Sand Dunes. We visited the jaw-dropping Grand Canyon. We explored the Pictured Rocks National Lakeshore in the Upper Peninsula in Michigan.

The visit that year that stands out the most was Cuyahoga Valley National Park in Ohio, right outside of Cleveland. On the day that we went, the cicadas were releasing from their 17-year sleep, and the sound was like nothing you could ever imagine. If you think about the sound of cicadas on a warm summer evening, multiply that by millions! It is only once every 17 years that the cicadas release in this fashion. If you looked up, they were buzzing around everywhere, and the noise was like a loud motorboat with no boat in sight. They covered the ground. It was surreal. We hiked and listened and watched in complete awe. It was something that all of us will remember forever. The idea that a cicada sleeps underground for 17 years and then emerges for a short time to do its living on earth only to then die is a science lesson worth the wait. Each of these trips was so different. The beauty of the experience was overwhelming. To share these experiences with your children is priceless.

I feel that parenting is an equal part of holding on and letting go all throughout the journey. It's a red flag to me with anyone who disassociates with their children. To have deep connections with your children is the greatest gift of all.

Chapter 5

Never Stop Exploring

"Expand your view and see the world through a different lens."

I truly enjoy a good adventure and getting off the beaten path. I especially appreciate these experiences with my children and nieces, who are all young adults now. Perhaps it is because I love the blissful ignorance of youth. Just take me to a place and give me a path, and that is all I need. We have some great conversations on the hiking trails about life.

When I was a young adult, we had our fair share of adventures. In college, I had a tight group of friends with similar beliefs, a passion for a good road trip, and hand-me-down cars that gave us a portal to the open road. So, we went. It started one year with an impromptu road trip to New York City to see the ball drop in Times Square. You only need to do this once in your lifetime.

We packed the cars with garbage bags full of our clothes, snacks because we were too poor to get food along the way, and a little bit of cash for necessities like gas and tolls. The highway along Ohio and Pennsylvania seemed endless, but we finally rolled into New Jersey, where we slept on the floor of our friends' parents' house. We drove into New York City the next day and visited Central Park, the Brooklyn Bridge, and had a long-distance view of the Statue of Liberty. It was December, so it was cold, and the trees were empty. We were not adequately dressed for staying out all night for the ball drop. Regardless, our spirits were filled with the cold air, the joy of being in a new place, and an once-in-a-lifetime adventure.

We made it to Times Square, and we stood for hours, breathing in the atmosphere of all that is new in the big city. It was the holiday season, so the lights gleamed in all different colors. A few snow-flakes fell and whirled around in the windy air.

A new year signifies a fresh start. People stood close and rooted for the new beginning. After several hours, our fingers were numb, and our bones were rightly chilled. I remember see-ing Dick Clark from very far away, and when he talked, the crowd roared. There was music, but we were so far away I couldn't even see who the artists were. As we got closer to midnight, the energy of the people around us grew. The countdown began, and a new year was ushered in. We were so cold that almost immediately, we made the way to our car to blast the heat and warm our cold but reju-venated souls.

Our adventures continued. San Diego, Tijuana, Mexico, the Grand Canyon, and Washington DC made the short list. When we graduated from college, our destination was Oregon. We spent several days in the mountains and a few more hiking the coast. Our young selves really had no idea how to manage a back-woods mountain camping trip, but we used our best judgment and tried to make good choices. The three sister's mountain range was our goal.

We hiked several miles to our campsite. Leaving notes at the trailhead in case we came up missing, met some hungry bears or got hurt. Although that sounds extreme, this was a time before cell phones, fit-bit watches, or other tracking mechanisms that could quickly pinpoint missing people. All we had was a paper map and we were young and pretty inexperienced campers. We thought we owned the world, though.

Imagine hiking up to 10 miles in the deep woods with a 30-pound backpack. We had a blast. We sang songs and talked nonsense most of the way. The wildlife was out and about as it was May and getting warmer by the day. There was still snow on the mountain tops that we could see along our hike. We found our campsite and put up our tents. All of our backpacks held our food, and so we needed to hoist them into a tree high up to avoid bears and other animals getting to them. Our pulley and hoist method worked like a charm.

The next morning was frigid. So we moved slowly until mid-morning, making coffee and breakfast over the campfire. The climb up the mountain didn't look too far, so we felt good about our time. It was slowly getting warmer, too. So we headed upwards in great stride. The hike was gorgeous and we made it to the top in time for dinner. Uh-oh, not enough time to get down before dark. So, we improvised. At the mountain peak, it was snowy, so we cut up garbage bags and used them as slides to scoot down the mountain in no time. We found out later that these were glaciers and we could've been lost in a deadly crevasse. Maybe that wasn't the best move, but that is my point.

In our youth, we sometimes take risks out of a lack of understanding and experience. These are what memories are made of. That is why I love traveling with the young adults in my family; they bring along that zest for fun and risk that I might not take at my age. That's why when we hike, we talk about who takes what role in the event of an emergency.

If I fell off this cliff, where are the car keys and money? *Who would go for help? Who takes the lead?* We laugh about it mostly, but it also helps us to face the mortality of our adventure. As kids grow older, they have more in-depth and philosophical conversations, which I particularly enjoy. Like me when I was young, some of our talks are just plain nonsense.

I love trees. One year my daughter and I went to Philadelphia for a conference. We visited the museum where Rocky climbed the steps to victory. The museum had a photography exhibit on people who climbed the enormous trees in Sequoia National Park. I had to go there and see those trees.

The next year, we hopped off a plane at LAX with a dream and a cardigan and went to Sequoia

National Park. Our first stop was to climb Morro Rock. This huge boulder sits high up on the mountain range and you can climb to what seems like the heavens. It was August and the blue sky was deep as we climbed the mountain and eventually up Morro Rock. Since I had the keys, money and a more risk averse age, I let the kids make the summit to the top. I stayed at a more reasonable elevation. They hollered along the way so I would know they didn't fall to their demise. The California view from the top of Morro Rock was beautiful, as I could see from their cell phone photographs.

Then we made our way the next day to see the gigantic trees. I am so serious when I say that I have never seen anything like it − these trees. I've even seen the California Redwoods, and the sequoias just blow your mind. You drive through the winding roads of the park. Take a sharp turn and you enter a world that doesn't even seem real. It is a must-see because there are no words to explain the statuesque trees that occupy this land. We were in awe! We walked with our heads looking up and up along the trails of miles of ancient sequoias. We hugged those trees that looked like they might swallow us whole. There was a path where you are most likely to see bears and so the youthful energy of our group led us in that direction. We saw a group of people huddled and pointing. It was a herd of bears. Two or three and they seemed smaller like they might be just cubs. The kids walked closer and closer. We discussed the "bear protocol." What do you do if a bear charges you? Stay calm, slowly retreat with hands over your head, low tone of voice is what Google says and what I reiterated to them.

Those young kids got super close to the bears, but we refrained from getting so close to petting them. On the way off the trail, we ran into a deer. My niece is afraid of a deer but got up close and personal with the bear. This is the reason I love to travel with young people. Go to Sequoia National Park in California, and it will amaze you to no end.

When you look at some of the oldest trees in the world, you realize how big the world is and how small you are; all around you is a feeling of deep connection with all things living and natural. Nature doesn't judge, but those bears might.

Another great wonder of natural beauty is Utah. I never thought twice about Utah until my best friend suggested it for my 50th birthday. So, we went. This was right when COVID-19 hit the United States. It was getting trickier to travel; however, we were able to get the trip in just prior to the world shutting down. I love the desert southwest as a general rule and Utah did not disappoint. We visited Arches National Park, Canyonlands and Zion. All of which meet your wildest expectations when it comes to the beauty and majesty of the natural space. In Zion we went glamping, which is just fancy camping with beds, bathrooms in the tent, coffee service and gourmet food—not like when I was 20 years old and huffing into the woods for ten miles with a backpack. This is the glory of age, experience and financial independence. The view from our tent was the majestic red rocks of Utah.

We hiked the Wildcat Trail to Northgate Peak, and our conversation had me rolling with laughter. After discussing the emergency plan if I (the carrier of the keys and holder of the money) fell off a cliff and a bobcat protocol if suddenly one presented itself on the trail, we moved on to other matters. The lighter trail talk was that tent showers were disrespectful and that strawberry-flavored water hits just right.

Then we talked about how regret is a choice and the idea of reincarnation. We decided together that it was important to be a good person so you don't come back in the next life as something terrible. My niece came out of the womb knowing she was a boy in her past life and we all believed her. We wondered if animals have regret or feel anticipation. Like those cicadas that live in the ground for 17 years then emerge and die so quickly. Were they awake those 17 years with the anticipation of seeing the earth and coming out of the ground? These are the types of conversations I adore on the hiking trail. In addition to those moments of beauty and contemplation, that we are here, present and with each other. We are presented with many paths in life, so choose them wisely and appreciate the ebbs and flows as you navigate, because one day you will look back and realize the life in between.

One of my personal goals in this life is to be a good role model for young people. In my travels with my kids and family, I especially enjoy the time spent having deep conversations and making memories together. More than anything else, I appreciate passing along the love of nature that I have because it can heal the weary soul and provide a perspective that is spiritual and deep. Find those connections in your life and hold on to them. Look for ways to have peace and find solace and then do it. Do it often and then share it with those who might also benefit from it. It builds strength in ourselves and in those we love.

Chapter 6

On Romance

"Great love is all around us if only we choose to see it."

When I was in college, I took a Women's Study class that changed my perspective forever. Although I learned many important nuggets of information, there are two in particular that shaped my life from that moment on. As women, we should always have financial and emotional independence. This means making your own money and being able to afford your own lifestyle, regardless of having a significant other. Also, know and love yourself before involving anyone else. If you seek other people for validation, you will always be looking. Validate yourself first. We may not want to admit it but this is a super hard lesson for women. Always one that we have to remind ourselves of. It is so easy to get distracted.

Throughout this class, there was much discussion about relationships. I found myself wondering if we were meant to have different relationships at different phases of our lives. Were couples REALLY meant to stay together for a lifetime? I was raised in a very traditional Catholic family, so the answer up until that moment was yes.

My first love was in high school and spanned through my first few years of college. It wasn't an overwhelming love; pretty normal and unevent-ful in hindsight. My mother never thought he was good enough, and I spent my time seeking valida-tion and trying to please him.

It is part of my hopeful spirit that always finds me holding on for too long. After about seven years, we finally split up for good. I spent a few years growing my career and dating around but with nothing serious on the horizon.

Somewhere in my mid-twenties, that biological clock started ticking louder and louder. Although I spent much time up until this point saying I didn't want children, the clock started to beat consistently and strongly and eventually became deafening. I remember working in a homeless shelter, and one day this man got off the elevator for a meeting with me. I remember what he was wearing to this day. We got to know each other, dated, lived together, became engaged, and one day got married. Our outdoor ceremony was on a beautiful day in September. It was a mixture of poetry, acoustic guitar, and a hand-picked flower arrangement right from the botanical garden—All the friends and family surrounding our good wishes. When I got married, there was a small voice in the back of my head saying, "hmmm, I wonder if he is really the one."

I always said that I married him for his features, which was a joke, but maybe not wholly.

He had jet black hair and deep brown eyes that I thought would make beautiful children and they did. Within a couple of years, we had our son. He came out of the womb with the deepest, darkest locks of hair you could ever imagine. In the grocery store, people would say that he is too pretty to be a boy. Still to this day, I don't really know what that meant, but he had stunning features.

So often, when people begin to build a life together, they have the traditional ideas of marriage that may be a tad unrealistic. Like somehow, if you find the right person, it will all be so easy. One thinks about Disney movies, Hallmark Christmas shows, or even their own traditional marriages in their family. They are all over the place. But the truth of the matter is that marriage is hard.

First, there seems to be insurmountable expectations. Expectations of how the relationship will function and how the other person will be. I realize that people evolve over time, but as a general rule, the personality traits you have are the ones that you'll die with. As women, sometimes we think we can fix them, they will change for us or that we can get them to change. That is the first myth. Entering into marriage thinking that we're going to fix or change them is simply not how it works. People are people. The good and bad come along with them. It is important to see people and take them for who they are. Otherwise, we are fooling ourselves and making the situation harder on everyone.

If you have children, another expectation revolves around parenting. If you think marriage is hard, try entering parenting into the mix. Please understand that parenting is one of the greatest joys I've had in my lifetime. So, this part is not a referendum on the downfall of the family dynamic. Simply put, when you are expecting a grown human to change and then you add a baby into the mix with the exhaustion, uncertainty, and stress; it amplifies the challenge to a level that many simply cannot grow accustomed to. Whether in a marriage or not, the burden of parenting is great and the importance of doing it well is underestimated.

Although the traditions of what we saw in marriage and parenting were the same, the approaches we decided to take were different. There were differences in spirituality and religion. Being raised Catholic, there were expectations from the start as to what that would look like. There was little agreement. Ultimately, we decided to let our children decide for themselves as they grew into adults. That said, our children were introduced to Catholicism by going to family weddings and funerals of those who fell in line with these traditions. They were introduced to Buddhism and the many aspects of this spiritual path. We talked with our kids about what it means to be an atheist. Our children would have a more diverse understanding of multiple aspects of religion and spirituality than most.

I knew I was going to be a working mother. Which meant there were dividing lines in marriage and parenting that made this a challenge too. I felt continually judged about having the children in daycare, taking meetings, going to work on their days off or just abandoning them in general.

If you are going to be a working mom, find a true and equal partner for a significant other. One who takes a generous portion of the responsibility and judgment along with you? I cannot underscore this enough.

My expectation in getting married was that it would generally be a happy experience. Having a partner to share life with, have and raise children with, and experience the joy and pain of what life has to offer. What I didn't spend enough time thinking about was the type of partner that compliments and balances you when you are hurting, struggling or during significant loss. We all experience these moments. No one goes without them, not a single person. If the person you are with is dismissive during these times, doesn't help you get through them or leaves you to drown in what you are going through, it is not the right person. Try to always be the balance with your partner, during good and bad, just like the traditional vows tell us.

It is during these times that you learn the strength of your bond. Or, similarly, the weakness.

It can be the tipping point to a marriage. You have to learn how to rebound from these times, or the bond can disintegrate. I know that sometimes at work, I get bored and frustrated. It seems extra hard to stay motivated and engaged. I end up spending time being out of focus and less productive; my heart just isn't in it in the same way. Then I find some new program or part of my job that sparks my passion once again and brings me back to "center."

I wonder if this is the same type of process that helps marriages and relationships during difficult times. We need ways to come back to "center" and find the passion again, over and over. This is how we create longevity and stability. We also need to be flexible and adaptable.

Let's face it, most people like a good routine. They like security and little change. In reality, our lives are always changing and evolving; even though as people we hate that. Being adaptable to those changes as we move through the stories of our lives is critically important. If there is no adaptability, there will be complacency. Where there is complacency, there is death. So, we must be careful of our expectations of each other. I'm not suggesting a complete lack of standards when dealing with other people. We must meet people where they are and accept them for their good and bad because we are not perfect. We are human— Keep our expectations to their most basic: respect, honesty, and equality. This, in and of itself, is a tall order for some.

Some marriages last a lifetime, and some do not. I wonder if those marriages that have found longevity have happiness. My guess is that it is a mixture. It's like when you are a kid. All you want is to grow up and become an adult do whatever you want. Then you grow up and think how easy it was to be a kid. The grass isn't always greener on the other side. It's greener on the side you water. So, water those relationships well and they will flourish.

My marriage ended in divorce. It was one of the hardest times of my life because I felt like a failure and I felt judged by those staunch traditionalists. I made the best of it and got through it.

I gained a stronger spirit and frame of mind as it relates to relationships.

In the first real relationship after the divorce (after the short-lived and rebound ones), I tried to evolve and not make the same mistakes twice. It was a relationship that developed during COVID-19, and we worked to keep our expectations minimal (respect, honesty, equality). It was one of the deepest connections I've ever experienced. During COVID-19, you couldn't really date in a traditional manner. We focused on cooking together, having long talks, deep conversations and exploring our dreams and passions. Our lives molded together nicely, although it was not perfect. Instead of going out on dates, expecting fancy dinners and being higher maintenance; we looked to the simple joys in life and bonded together. Our interests had many layers; we knew each other well over time.

Finding people to truly relate to on a deeply personal level is very much a gift. It is done by reducing our expectations, finding common ground, enjoying the simple moments, balancing each other during difficult times and being adapt-able. I love *love* and all the anticipation that goes along with it. I seek those who love with their whole self and with no regret. This love can be found in friendships, in a partner, between mothers and children, siblings and should be held on to for dear life. As it is what life is made of?

Chapter 7

For the Love of Winter

"You need the depths of winter to appreciate spring."

I am a creature of winter. I don't really know how it happened because when I was young, I used to get really depressed after Christmas. That long stretch between January and springtime just felt like an eternity. As a result, I began to create ways to enjoy the little things about winter. The first snowfall or the fact that many of my family members have birthdays in winter. So, there is an abundance of cake during this time. I am a modest person. So I love being clothed from head to toe with sweaters, boots, scarves, wool socks and everything in between. I hate the heat of summer, my least favorite season. Not to mention I was born in winter, an Aquarius to be exact, which may mean something to some of you.

My favorite birthday story and one reason why I appreciate the depths of winter is when my little brother was born. It was in December of 1974 and there was a blizzard. I recall old photographs of my older brother and me in our snowmobile suits of fabulous 1970 color with snow that towered over our heads. We would go out onto the creek when the ice was safe and build forts into the snow drifts. It was like a dream.

The street we lived on was a one-lane, dead-end road that was really only traveled by us who lived there, so inevitably, it was the last street in the county to get plowed. That happened to be the case during the blizzard of 1974. My mom was nine months pregnant and went into labor as the snow fell, and her options were grim. She wasn't the type of woman who wanted an at-home birth, so out-of-the-box thinking was required.

Our family was in the farming business, so tractors were at our disposal, and my mom was getting more anxious to get to the hospital. My dad called upon his brothers to bring a large tractor to get her out and to the local hospital. It probably seems pretty old-fashioned but imagine a young mother at nine months of pregnancy hobbling out to jump on the John Deere to catch a ride to the hospital and give birth, but that is exactly how it played out. My dad obviously went with her.

For my brother and I, we got a trip across the creek to our aunt and uncle's house. My uncle came over to drop off the tractor and took my brother and me across the creek to stay with them until the storm was over and my new sibling arrived. I don't recall how long it was, but this is my first real memory of winter and a beloved story in our family. Even today, we'd likely have to use the same method for getting out during a snowstorm. Few even know our road exists, and that is how we like it.

The idea of hibernation also reminds me of winter. We could take a lesson from animals who hibernate and slow their metabolism during the cold months. When the time changes in November and the light goes down too early, there's a strange feeling that sets in that I think in my mind is like when hibernation sets in. Your biological clock just slows down and feels like a long winter's nap. I have learned to love this about winter.

As my kids grew up, I instilled in them a joyfulness towards the cold season. We spent time outdoors enjoying the cold, the snow, and the overall beauty of the season. To this day, we take an annual ski trip to enjoy our time together while breathing in the cold air. My ancestors are German, and we were always taught, (although I don't know how much of this is true), that getting cold air in your lungs is really healthy. So, I impress this upon my kids too and we get outdoors to enjoy winter getting as much cold air in our lungs as we can stand.

In January of 2017, we made our way to the largest women's march in history. Our travels took us to Washington DC, but there were women's marches held on the same day all across America and throughout the world. It was an epic day in history and I made darn well that my kids and I were a part of it. Leaving from Michigan, we stopped along the Ohio and Pennsylvania Turnpikes. Groups of women with signs and bumper stickers in their windows and their hearts full of purpose were also making their way. The energy was full of support and a mission for a purpose greater than ourselves— for our mothers, daughters, aunts and sisters. My son came along as well; I feel like our feminist household rubbed off on him a tad over the years.

We made it to DC and after a good sleep, we woke before the sun and started to make our way to the rally. From the first metro stop, lines and lines of women and men gathered. Signs in their hands and purpose in their hearts. On the metro, we all laughed, talked and had amazing synergy for the day. A group of girls from Northern Michigan University in Marquette sat next to us and we made small talk about our great state. Getting off the metro, it was unseasonably warm for January. The amazing number of people was overwhelming and we loved reading the variety of signs that appeared.

To march in a rally on the National Mall in Washington DC, is an experience not to forget. To walk in THIS march was beyond anything we could've imagined. There were hundreds of thousands of women, men, and children all convening in support of one another to rise against old-fashioned ideologies and sexism. I've never been in such a large crowd, but also never felt so safe in my life. People were kind. People were expressing their power and in all that, there was a feeling of solidarity that I had never felt before. I knew none of them but understood all of them.

To teach your kids what it means to stand up for what you believe in and to KNOW what you would speak up loud and proud for, is a true gift of parenting. To allow them to experience solidarity on purpose is magical. That is what this trip meant for us. The drive home in January on the Pennsylvania Turnpike was nothing but treacherous, but I love a good snowy challenge and we made it home safe. The experience forever changed our lives.

Know what it is that you stand for and what you'll stand up for. Deeply rooted values are developed from birth and throughout generations. Take the time to explore your own values and stand firm on your ground. Not everyone will appreciate the ground you stand on, but that is not the point. Having deep connections and strong values makes for a life that is bigger than just ourselves. Some people miss that in living their day-to-day lives, they don't have time to give thought to the ground that they stand on and what is really important to them. Once you find it, teach your kids how to find theirs and help them feel solidarity. For those who might not appreciate your solid ground, build a bridge of understanding. It takes all of us to make the world a better place.

Chapter 8

The Simple Things

"Each moment is special."

This is a story about paying attention to the simple things. Don't get me wrong, there's something to say for the grandiose gesture. I feel there's strength in understanding and appreciating the little moments we have in life. Holding onto them to make our everyday bright. So often, people let the little moments pass right by them without even noticing, but if we look a little deeper at the little ones, it helps bring more joy to our lives.

Let's start with our obsession with the gran-
diose gesture. For me, the big deal is just way too
much; I'm not one who needs a lot of attention.
Behind the scenes is where I'd prefer to be. When I
turned the beautiful age of 40, a great celebration
was planned. The friends were invited. A tour bus
was rented that we all loaded on to. We visited many
of my lifetime spaces...the house where I grew up...
my first real job.where I went to college.where my
kids were born. There was delicious food and my
favorite cake. A video compilation of my life thus
far. Even ended in a firework show. A grandiose
gesture for sure.

But to know me is to know that I wasn't
really comfortable with all that attention. That is
not to say I didn't appreciate the gesture, but it was
all too much pressure. I recall one of my dearest
friends coming to me a few days later explaining
how she thought it was just all NOT ME because
I revel in the simple things that make me happy.
What I remember most of that night is after the
party, I sat down with my best wine in hand and

watched one of my favorite movies with my kids (and maybe my cat) draped over my lap.

In this world, I'm afraid we are always awaiting the grandiose gesture, and we end up giving the simple joys away. We miss the everyday joys of what brings solace and happiness. I try every day to recognize those moments and bring them to the forefront to shine. In Costa Rica, they have a phrase that exemplifies their way of life, "Pura Vida," meaning the pure life or the simple life. It is a phrase that takes hold in their everyday living, making it seem almost like another planet. Many of us have gotten too far away from the simple life, so here is a worthy reminder, should you choose to accept it.

Although summer is not my best season, there is something to say for summer days when you open the doors and windows of your house. Maybe it is the idea that you've finally made it through the long winter and the fresh breeze blows in new life to a stale space. When those windows open, pay attention to kids laughing and playing outside. It is the pure sound of childhood and the freedom only a beautiful summer day can offer to a kid without a care in the world.

However, I also realize that kids and adults, for that matter, don't always walk around that carefree anymore. There are pressures on everyone, self-created or completely out of their control, that shape our days, thoughts and our minds. I'm not oblivious to our complicated lives, but I also feel that some of it is self-perpetuated. We feel like we need to be busy all the time. I see kids who go from school to sports to work to study with no end in sight. I see adults work a full day, work out and make dinner only to put their kids to bed in sheer exhaustion. In between, we check our emails and scroll our social media. Only to watch other people doing more and that makes us feel bad about our pace. Let's try to stop and breathe.

This is where it is important to get to know people. Paying attention to the little things that bring joy to OUR OWN lives is one task and yet another is getting to know those who are around us. Then once we know them, use that knowledge to spread some happiness. It makes the world around us better and richer. Not in money, but in love. Because when someone knows that you've paid enough attention to know them and do the things that make them happy, it can change the world. At least your little chunk of it.

Think about the smells that you love. Pine trees in the rain, chocolate chip cookies baking and fresh-cut grass. These are a few of mine – and everyone has them. On Christmas morning in our house, we have a tradition of making fresh cinnamon rolls before the days' worth of family activity. So when anyone in my house smells cinnamon rolls, they think fondly of Christmas morning.

The concept is simple. Take the time to pay attention to the daily events that make people you care about happy. Then do them. When they are having a bad day, are sad or just need a pick-me-up do those things. It does wonders for the soul.

I have a friend whose kids go to Oxford High School and were there during the recent school shooting. The next day, she was wondering what to do for them. "Do things that make them feel normal," I said. Make cookies; the smell brings comfort. They took a walk on the winter trails and had a snowball fight. The little things make us feel normal when life is not.

This is not to minimize the horror of school shootings and the trauma and healing that need to go along with it. A mother knows what brings comfort to their children. Sometimes the comfort of normalcy is good for the psyche.

Depending on where you live, try to marvel at the seasons. I have favorite smells for each of them, which I don't love equally, but bring much joy. The smell of fresh-cut grass feeds my anal-retentive soul in the summer, a campfire and burning leaves in the fall help me to relax and unwind, a pine tree in the winter and cinnamon rolls mark the holiday season. The fresh air and spring flowers like daffodils and hyacinth tell of the renewal of spring.

THE SIMPLE THINGS

I'm always reminded of my dearest friends in the fall. We used to play a game called the "HA" game. I don't have any idea whose idea this was or where the game originated to give those props, but it is one of life's little pleasures for us. Imagine this....or better yet, try it out. Absolutely hilarious.

One person lies on the ground. The next person lays their head on the stomach of the other person already lying on the ground. Then the next person lays their head on the stomach of the last person who laid down, and so on and so forth. Then the first person says "HA," and then the next person joins in. Before long, everyone is laughing out loud. It's the easiest way to get people laughing at no cost and with no equipment. The simple things.

I inherited a beautiful old farmhouse from my grandparents. It is a labor of love and some days just simply a pain in my ass. My grandmother Irma loved her garden and had many varieties of beautiful flowers that popped up by surprise each spring and throughout the summer. She was very proud of her garden, and so when I moved into the home, I felt pressure to continue the garden's perfection. In the spring, the grass greens all around, the flowers perk up through the wet soil and the weeds have yet to take over. It's my best season in terms of the garden.

I grab bunches of spring varieties to breathe life back into the house with a sweet scent of wildflowers and the hope of springtime renewal. It is the legacy that my grandmother left for me and I try to appreciate it as all the blooms come alive.

Grandparents are important in our lives. Our parents give us the tools for a better life, but our grandparents shape us with their absolute and unconditional love. Get to know your grandparents and who they were before they are gone. I'll always remember how much I learned about my grandfather from his obituary. Time lost even though he lived two doors down.

My other grandmother taught us the love of coffee. Is there no better smell in the morning hours than your first cup of coffee? I have such vivid memories of my brother and me heading for a sleepover, and she would give us coffee with loads of cream and sugar. It's how I drink it to this day, and it makes me smile at her and the deep love she had for her grandchildren.

I could go on and on. But my point here is simple...pay attention to the little things in life that bring you joy and do them. Every day. Then share the love by learning what others around you enjoy as simple pleasures and do them too. These joys will improve your life and the lives of those you love. Happiness is contagious.

Chapter 9

In the Company of Women

"Building unbreakable bonds."

I am a self-proclaimed feminist. I wasn't raised this way; it came along as I followed my path through life. However, I have always been surrounded by strong women. Not the bra burning, ladder-climbing or break the glass ceiling kind. The kind who keeps a quiet, constant presence in your life and shapes you throughout your time here. For me, this is my mother, grandmothers, relatives, friends and my daughter. This story is for them.

My grandmothers were both housewives. Their job was to raise the family. They kept up the home and provided love to the family while my grandfathers worked and made a living. This was a time when there was only one car in the driveway. The home was modest yet comfortable and dinner time was sacred.

My grandma Skippy was a great joy in my life. She had out-of-date ideas and had no idea how to take me and my feminists' rants when I would come home from college and visit her. She was a woman who loved me unconditionally until the day she died and I know she watches over me to this day. On my mom's side of my family, I was the only female grandchild, surrounded by five male cousins. One way for a girl to grow up tough is to surround her with a bunch of brothers and cousins who treat her like "one of the guys." We made some memories and Grandma Skippy was in the middle of all of them. Whether she was out in the back-yard pool with her polyester pants rolled up to her knees, while she waded through the water with us;

or playing checkers and rummy showing us creative ways to win (better known as cheating), I only found out later in life when playing in college. My grandma embraced every moment.

My grandma Irma was a tough German woman who loved to have her hands in the ground tending her garden. I can picture her vividly, hands behind her back, strolling the garden watching over her natural beauties, enjoying their perfection. Since she lived in the country, she kept strange outdoor pets like a crow and a raccoon but could chop off a chicken's head and dress that bird like nobody's business. She loved to paint and after she died I hung one of her paintings in my house. The home where she and my grandfather built, lived, and she died. She loved to convene all of us cousins for birthdays, holidays and the occasional snow day just to breathe life into the house. Gentle and soft-spoken, my grandma Irma was a special woman. It is important to recognize our grandmas and see them for the place they hold in our lives, just like our mothers.

Many people have challenging relationships with their mothers. I appreciate my mom for her approach to raising us and me as a young girl. Don't get me wrong, it wasn't always perfect, but she instilled in me some important lessons that shaped me into the woman I am today. My mom taught us never to circumvent our responsibility. If we were sick, she'd give us a minute and tell us to get back to it. If we took a sport or class of some type and we wanted to quit, she'd make us finish. She wasn't about telling us how perfect we were and she definitely was more of a disciplinarian. I always wanted to please both of my parents and never disappoint them, but my mom was very stern in her expectations of us. I was also the middle child in between two brothers, and being the only girl was special for her. She enrolled me in dance class, gymnastics. She took me to the hair salon, got me perms, and we loved to go shopping. She also was adamant that I not have premarital sex, have babies out of wedlock, drink, do drugs or date people not of my caliber. Sometimes she just plain scared the crap out of me.

So, I made it through high school and took a sigh of relief having met the expectations. Then the words "I'm 18 and I can do what I want" uttered from my lips. I changed course and went off to college.

At that time, more women were heading to college than ever before. Most of my female relatives and friends were heading to college, as was I. My best friend throughout childhood was my closest cousin. We were the same age and did so much together growing up due to us also being related. We spent holidays together, played sports and instruments together, had the same friends and had many sleepovers. I loved staying at her house because her mom (my aunt) made tacos, and that was not a dinner option in my household. She also had cable TV, where we would sit for hours watching MTV awaiting our favorite videos and songs. She was smarter and prettier than me, and I always made efforts to be more like her.

I guess as girls, at some point in our lives, we develop this natural tendency to compare ourselves to one another. Good or bad, right or wrong, sometimes this tendency lasts a lifetime if we don't learn how to check it at the door. It can lead to bad behavior. I didn't really acknowledge this until I went off the college; learned a few things and met some women that would change the unnecessary need to measure myself against anyone else but ME. This was such a pivotal moment for me in my evolution as a woman and a feminist. It helped me build stronger connections with women around me. My best friend in college helped me see how important bonds with women are throughout our lives. We made our fair share of fuck-you cassette tapes in college, lamenting the latest break-up. We wore our long johns, boxer shorts and wool socks to the grocery store in the middle of the night to get ice cream. We've gone to protests, explored beautiful places and supported each other's endeavors. We celebrated our weddings, births of our children, loss of a parent or sibling and we hold our friendship forever. This is all there is to it.

There are so many wonderful women who have shaped my life over the years, both personally and professionally. I am so very lucky for that. These women have shown me what it is like to put the measuring stick away and support each other. To build each other up instead of tearing one another down. So, when I had a daughter of my own, it was important for me to get it right. Raising a daughter to find her strength and confidence was important to me. It is only because of the women who shaped me that I was even up for the task.

My daughter was born on Mother's Day – a true and forever gift in my life. She and her older brother are my only two children. Like myself, we chose to raise our children in close proximity to our family, so they have always been very close to their cousins. Their first and likely lifetime friends. Teaching my daughter strength and confidence was something I didn't know how to do. So, I went back to my childhood and thought about how my mother and grandmothers raised me. They didn't raise me to be a feminist, so I wanted to change that for my daughter so she didn't have to begin at college to have exposure to women's independence.

Let me take a step in here to say that even though I didn't learn about feminism and women's independence from those women in my life who came before me, I'm not blaming anyone. Generations change and evolve, and traditions grow and adapt over time; my family is not unique in this way. My mother and grandmothers were neither feminists nor independent, and there's nothing wrong with that. But for me, what I wanted for my daughter, was to pass along emotional and financial freedom. When women have emotional and financial freedom, the world is a better place. It also changes the viewpoint from which we see men in our lives. True partnerships can exist where there is emotional and financial freedom to allow them to be so. These are the gifts I wanted to share with my daughter. But how do you do that?

The real truth of the matter is that when I gave birth to my daughter, I didn't have emotional freedom. It was only when I released myself from MY emotional struggles that she truly saw a model of what that was like. As a working mom, I was always a professional in her eyes. I made my own money, had my own career, and financial freedom was in place. I was in an emotional state in my marriage that simply wasn't working and I'd be lying if I said that my children couldn't see that. Once I gained my emotional freedom, it was like a window opened. After gathering my emotional strength, I watched my daughter grow into her own. She volunteered for a Congressional campaign and came out of her shell. Surrounded by young, vibrant and smart women. We joined a Huddle Group of women with similar philosophies and supportive ways that give comfort on days when you need it most. I trust she understands how important it is to put the measuring stick away, build your own confidence in self-love and create support for other women that is above all else.

Suffice it to say that I am not a perfect human being, so I still get into it with women every now and again. I still protest against the inequities that we all face but realize that there are moments when I am part of the problem and not the solution. I try to get better and be better for the women around me. That starts with my daughter. We have a terrific bond, one that led her to write the foreword of this book. She knows it was on my bucket list and supports me every day in reaching MY dreams. I also assist her in reaching for the stars, breaking the glass ceiling and becoming her true self. I always say that parenting is equal parts holding on and letting go. I hope more than anything else that I've given her the tools to be a good, strong, kind and independent woman.

If I've done that, then it'll be alright.

I have this beautiful friend who is a mentor for young girls. She does a mirror project with them. When we look at ourselves in the mirror, especially those awful close-up ones you find in hotel rooms, what do we see? It is so easy for us to see the blemishes, imperfections, and the negative. We put the mirror down and walk away. Let's flip that narrative. Look at yourself and see those wrinkles and know it resembles a life well-lived. When we see the dark circles, it is the sleeplessness of passion.

I heard this saying once that nature, unlike us, never apologizes for its beauty. Let's stop apologizing.

Chapter 10

The View From Here

"This is what it's like to fall backward."

Admittedly, I had it pretty good growing up. In the grand scheme of things, I was extremely lucky. My parents were grounded, loving and provided everything we needed and more. We lived in our family home my entire childhood. On a one-lane dead-end street that most people didn't even know existed. Our house included a farm, as that was part of our extended family business. We were in tune with the planting season in spring and I could name crops in fields, know what a plow is and its purpose and what a harvest moon is all about.

Our house was along the family woods, where we spent our days exploring both wildlife and wildflowers (and poison ivy), building tree forts from fallen victims and roaming along the stream. It is where I learned to identify our state wildflower, the trillium, notice the massive spread of an eagle's nest and heard the quaint call of owls while I slept. This is where the spring bloomed, the summer turned green and the fall leaves fell like snow. I developed a love of nature that brings deep solace to me by simply wandering the familiar trails of those woods.

We also lived on a large creek, so we had water at our disposal that ran directly into one of the Michigan Great Lakes. Some of my fondest young memories include wandering along the creek when the east wind blows and all the water flows out into the lake, leaving a muddy shoreline trail where my brothers and I would catch crawfish and pick up old, mucky bottles for fun. It may not seem like much fun in my older brain, but it was how we spent our time in childhood, with little care in the world, beautiful surroundings and people who loved us.

Within a one-mile radius of my childhood home were countless aunts, uncles, grandparents, cousins and more extended family than might feel normal. Whether it was a random snow day in the winter or a perfect mid-summer day, we always found each other and had a worthwhile adventure. My cousins all were in similar age ranges, so we gathered somewhere and spent the day outside having random fun, riding our bikes from all corners of our world.

Our family experienced losses, as all families do. Death, divorce, sickness and other matters help us to develop coping mechanisms for the changes that life has in store. It was pretty unspectacular for the most part but solid as a rock. Needless to say, when I graduated from high school, I wanted to get out and find bigger, better and more exciting things. It is only later in life that

I realize how that stable grounding in childhood prepared me for a meaningful life full of deeper connections. Like everyone, I have invisible walls that no one can see. They've come from a lifetime of experience.

At some point in college, I realized I wanted to chart my own path and grew the empowerment within to do so. I loved Northern Michigan, so when I graduated from the university, I took a road trip to a small lake town up north. It was one of my favorite destinations with a beautiful bay, small-town charm and glorious winters. I grabbed a local newspaper and went to eat lunch at the Big Boy. This was the time when newspapers contained everything a small town needed to know. Apartments to rent, jobs that were available and all the local gossip. So, I sat in that restaurant and circled apartments, jobs and interesting activities of daily life. That same day, I visited an apartment and put down a deposit.

I circled a job, went home and sent my application in the mail (it was before email and online submissions), and in a week; I had a phone call for an interview. It was like magic, I got the job and unbeknownst to me, my career began. We packed up the truck with my belongings and I made my way to my new home. It was empowering and scary at the same time; picking up your life and putting it in another place to start over. Not that you are a different person, but you could be if you wanted to. That feeling is powerful.

I quickly realized that I was surrounded by new people. When you grow up in a large extended family as I did, trust was easy and pretty much automatic. That's a tricky proposition when you've moved and started over somewhere new. Automatic trust can be dangerous. So, as I navigated this new space, I had to create some boundaries for myself and learn to trust my instincts. However, instincts are not foolproof and there are plenty of fools out there to prove that. I probably ended up in some situations that could have ended in tragedy, but I leaned on my instincts well and only a few times has that proven to be hurtful.

Over time you develop a method for building trust, but it is only by creating walls do we keep our self-preservation. It is the walls that people climb to show value, effort and eventually trust. It is these walls that bring us the people we are destined to meet. Some bring us joy, some bring us pain, some teach us lessons and some never leave. But most do. Most of us have more people in our lives that come and go than come and stay. The ones who come and stay break down those walls of trust and find the deepness of your spirit that comes with longevity.

For those who come and go, there are walls of disappointment. I hate to be disappointed. Having high expectations can be a blessing and a curse. But when people enter your life, it means they've come to you for a reason. We usually don't know what those reasons are initially, but if you follow the path, eventually, the intention reveals itself. When something ends, it can be hurtful. When we hurt, we build walls. In these cases, I struggle to forgive.

The walls we create for ourselves make us feel protected and safe. They allow us to show people what we want, to have some control. There are days when I feel like I've built a moat around myself to keep my hopefulness and positivity. I have to remember that to find deeper connections; we must be vulnerable and let some people cross the mote and come beyond the walls. There are people but also experiences and adventures that we seek in life to make meaning. It's about taking some risks. How many people live their daily lives in a safe bubble, not going out beyond the mote, even though they have dreams of doing so much more? These walls can keep us prisoners to realizing our greatest hopes, dreams and love. So, get to know your walls and then recognize their role in your true life's path.

Some of my deepest disappointments have come through failure. But let's explore the process of failure for a minute. When we put our hearts into something...a relationship, a job, a book. We open the door to self-doubt. If it doesn't work, we see it as a failure. What if, in reality, failure is the fuel we need to persist? To try again in a different way. They say if first, you don't succeed, try and try again. If we've learned nothing else from COVID-19, it is that we need to be more ready and willing to adapt. This builds resilience in our spirit and a never-give-up attitude. By looking at failure in a different way, we erase that invisible barrier for us to achieve. It is only an obstacle; it is not the end.

I have a project at work that I've been laboring on for more than eight years. I have learned more than I ever thought I would. It has cost money, energy and time and hasn't worked out the way I wanted. Yet. I have tried a series of different techniques to get this project off the ground. Each technique is a process where I learn and grow. However, it hasn't worked to achieve the results. When I realize that a technique is not going to work, I stop, I reflect and then I wait. My dad always taught me that patience is a virtue. It is also VERY HARD sometimes to realize when it's time to pivot and hang on. Then when it is time, another opportunity presents itself and I gain the strength to try again. I know in my heart that one day this project will be complete and it will be part of my legacy. Until then, I hear my dad reminding me of patience.

Finding great love is a journey. When I reflect on the love in my life, I consider myself very lucky. That is not to say that heartbreak, loss and disappointment haven't been part of that journey because they most certainly have. To find great love is to adapt and evolve in an ever-changing world. People change, environments change and we must see the big picture of how people fit into our lives. It is painful sometimes because we get these ideas in our heads of how relationships should be, for better or worse. To have great love is to first be willing to take down the walls, second be able to recognize it and third be able to nurture it. This is hard because people are people. Hurt and pain make us emotional. We don't always act our best when we are highly emotional. Then some relationships end. We've all been in that place.

There are relationships in our lives that open our world to so much more. I have a saying that the world always protects me from the things I don't want to see. I trust that, but it can also be a gray space sometimes. I don't always know who is in it for the right reasons and I don't even try to figure that out at this point in my life. The world will protect me from the things that I don't want to see. Sometimes, there are these forces that join us along our journey that are undeniable and unstoppable. I have my walls, yes. I also trust that people, experiences and adventures come to us. We get to decide whether to let them in our life or not. Are the walls going to be penetrated? If they are, be open but not stupid. Always protect yourself and know that people are human. Know your boundaries and live comfortably in that space. Limits are instincts – it is the world protecting us from what we don't want to see. So many people don't recognize them. Sometimes, we justify moving those boundaries for one reason or another. Let's be honest; we do this a lot. That's okay because we need to always challenge ourselves. If we don't take the risk every now and again, we become a prisoner of those walls. If we don't go outside of that box and feel uncomfortable, we don't grow.

Please don't take this as advice to go haphazardly into the wind. Or do, as long as you know your limits and keep safety in mind. For example, I'm inspired by people who willingly jump out of a plane. Skydiving is not in any way, shape, or form on a list of experiences I need to have. People do it all the time to challenge themselves and entire businesses are built around activities such as these. Experiences like swimming with sharks or tight-rope walking come with great risk and some people feel the need to do them. Cool. I can live my entire life without jumping out of a plane and be in absolute bliss. So, I know my limits and boundaries and how to challenge myself outside of them, but some things just don't appeal to my adventurous spirit.

Live in knowing what you need and want and go relentlessly and unapologetically towards it. So many of us live in the space of need and not want. There should be a balance. We live our daily lives based on what we need and for some that is a struggle. I am not dismissing the barriers that people have to getting their needs met. Everyone has them, and some are deeper than others. Sometimes we focus so hard on what we think we need that we lose sight of what we want for our lives, and we never live past that. Strike a balance.

When people see me on the surface, I tend to present as a professional—reserved, diplomatic, maybe even somewhat cold and rigid. I put a smile on and walk through my day. Trying to exude confidence, strength, making decisions, and helping people along the way. It is almost a mask, like putting makeup on every day. It is the pretty we want people to see. Don't get me wrong; I've come to love that pretty. I know who I am and being a professional is part of the person I love. It is part of what makes me feel whole. In the end, that professionalism leads to me helping people and trying to make the world a better place. Although some days are difficult and there are obstacles along the way, I keep my eyes on that prize.

On the other hand, put me in the woods or on a trail lollygagging endlessly, head in the clouds breathing in that huge perspective that will shrink any problem that I think I have and cannot fix. Hair back, no make-up, one with nature because nature never judges and nor should we.

In wrapping up this book, I had a moment of fear and doubt. So, I took a break and decided to go on a hike. I looked up the best trails in the area. One was familiar; one said there was no parking lot, a trailhead you needed to find as there were no signs, but the best overlook you'd ever see should you get there. Which trail do you take? The familiar or the unknown. This is the first choice. I go towards the unknown trail and I park somewhere, not really knowing. I get out. I walk. I find what looks like the trail, so I follow the path. My head is wondering if this is the right way or should I turn around. I keep my head in the clouds and keep wandering. It is spring, so there are leaves on the ground. I hear the leaves rustling and know something is coming toward me. It is a dog running right in my direction. It could chew my arm off, so I wonder what type of weapon I might have if it is ferocious. The dog stops looking at me and moves along. I keep walking and the dog eventually visits again. Walks with me for a while and disappears. I smile from this random incident. The last bit is an uphill climb and opens to a beautiful and scenic view. It was all worth the risk. However, sometimes it won't be because we build ideas up in our head, and then they can turn out to be disappointing.

Below the surface, behind the walls, we are all a little rough around the edges. Let's embrace the edges. Behind the walls, we all have emotions, both good and bad. Let's allow ourselves to feel those emotions. Behind the walls, we all get to make choices such as, whom we let in, how we accept the events that happen in our lives, where we go and which path to choose.

Have a mind and heart free enough and brave enough to make those choices to bring people in, see what is necessary for us to see, and be who we are meant to be. Choose every day to put it all out there, so there are no regrets.

How We See

By Stephanie Zorn -Kasprzack

Take in the love that comes our way; it
opens the heart

Enjoy the snow; it makes everything sparkle

Respect the pain, as it brings us strength

Soak in the sun; it provides needed warmth

Take in the fear; it helps to refine us

Watch the fall leaves blow so we can let go

Feel the rain on your face; it is how we grow

Breathe in anticipation it makes us long for more

Let the tears roll because they are real

You see it's all in perspective and how we choose to see.

About the Author

Stephanie Zorn-Kasprzak grew up in Monroe, Michigan. A small town between Toledo and Detroit. After graduating high school, she attended college at Eastern Michigan University, earning her degree in Written Communication. Zorn-
Kasprzak has a great passion for a good cause and has spent her entire professional career working for non-profit organizations that make a difference

in her community. She received a graduate degree in Organizational Leadership and is currently the executive director of a community action agency. Additionally, she teaches at her alma mater, EMU.

A free spirit who loves to get outdoors, Zorn-Kasprzak finds solace in nature and loves to travel and see all the beautiful spaces she can. She is deeply rooted in family, nature, and finding the beauty in life. She does this with her two children, who are the greatest joys of her life. One of her long-term personal goals is to be a good role model for children, so she volunteers as a mentor and coach and tries to empower youth in every aspect of her life. A daily yoga practice keeps her centered and mindful. It is a bucket-list goal to write a book, so here we go!

Made in the USA
Columbia, SC
30 July 2022